to Tommy

from,
Karen xxx

St Andrews
in old picture postcards

Eric Simpson

European Library ZALTBOMMEL / THE NETHERLANDS

Cover picture:

Shows the Step Rock Swimming Pool around 1930.

GB ISBN 90 288 6668 x

© 2001 European Library – Zaltbommel/The Netherlands

      Eric Simpson

No part of this book may be reproduced in any form, by print, photoprint, microfilm or any other means, without written permission from the publisher.

The moral right of the author has been asserted

European Library

post office box 49

NL – 5300 AA Zaltbommel/The Netherlands

telephone: 0031 418 513144

fax: 0031 418 515515

e-mail:publisher@eurobib.nl

Introduction

For this book I have selected old postcards and some photographs which reflect different aspects of St Andrews' past from the 19th century until the 1960s. The game of golf and its vital importance to the burgh is obviously one facet that cannot be ignored. Since, however, that sport and other aspects of the visual history of the town, including the role of the town's pioneer photographers, have been covered by others, I have, therefore, chosen to concentrate on an aspect which has not always received the attention it merits – namely the town's wider history as an all-round tourist resort. The burgh's development in the 18th and 19th centuries as a middle-class watering place and golfing Mecca is the starting point. Then we see how the town, remarkably without losing its traditional image, was successfully transformed into a semi-popular seaside resort. Postcards, sold in large numbers by Valentine's of Dundee and other publishers, illustrate the town's rise to prominence as a holiday resort and, at the same time, underline the very significant role that tourism has played in the history of this royal and ancient city. This story commences in the late 18th century with two aristocratic fashions, golf most obviously but, not less significant, a newer craze: the fad for sea bathing as a health cure for a variety of ailments both real and imaginary. It was this new medical fashion, the 'salt water cure', and the 'discovery', too, of the health-giving qualities of sea air that sparked off the rise of the seaside tourist industry.

It is evident from a document presented to the Town Council in 1784 that St Andrews was on its way to becoming a recognized seaside watering place. It contained a plea from some local notabilities, including three medical men, for the erection of 'a proper bathing-house', since the city had 'been much Resorted to, for some years past, by many Persons from the Country around for the Benefit of Sea Bathing.' There is no indication that such a changing facility was ever built. In those days, the dooking areas were segregated, males separated from females. Already by the early 1800s the Ladies Lake, west of the castle, was established as a ladies' bathing station. By there in 1810 a Captain Jackson built marine baths supplying hot and cold sea-water, thus permitting convalescents and less hardy dookers to bathe indoors and thereby avoid what one writer described as 'the disagreeables connected in a plunge on the open beach.' These 'Public Baths' also included rooms to let for 'company frequenting St Andrews in the bathing season'. But a writer in 1822 sadly remarked that these 'commodious and even elegant' baths were not a financial success. The boom time for St Andrews had yet to come. Until the railway age St Andrews was off the beaten track. Notwithstanding its historic ruins and ancient buildings, the town was isolated also in terms of contemporary cultural fashion. Had Sir Walter Scott been a golf aficionado, it would have been a different story. While Scott's magic pen sent tourists flocking to the Borders and to the Trossachs, it drew, in St Andrews' case, a virtual blank.

St Andrews, though, had the inestimable advantage of matchless golfing facilities and the support of a local population for whom, as Lord Cockburn observed in 1844, the game was 'not a mere pastime, but a business and a passion.' The contemporary parish clergy gave it their approval: 'The amusement of golf … is the best prophylactic in preventing dyspepsia and hypochondriasis.' Although, however, some settlers were attracted to the town for its golf and also for its schools and University colleges, visitors who played golf were not all that numerous. At that time, probably more people came to bathe than to golf. Roger in his *History of St Andrews* (1849) remarked on 'the occasional visits of noblemen and persons of eminence and wealth' attracted by 'the fine golfing ground'. The bathers, on the other hand, were not just from the patrician class, but were 'people of every description'. In late years, he added, their numbers had been 'very considerably on the increase.' A decade earlier, the Revd. Dr. Grierson had remarked on the elegant new houses that were 'generally well filled during that season when invalids and hypochondriacs lave their limbs in the briny deep'. Golf unfortunately was then an unduly expensive sport. For most visitors to the town, it had curiosity value only, the red-coated golfers of the social elite being regarded as one of the local sights. The turning point for the game of golf came in the late 1840s with the replacement of the very expensive-to-make featherie golf ball with the cheaper and longer-lasting guttie. This innovation coincided with the opening in 1847 of Leuchars railway station, which was followed in 1852 with the completion of the branch line to St Andrews. It is no coincidence that the Royal and Ancient started their new clubhouse in the following year. In time golf's popularity grew first in Scotland and then, with the golf boom of the 1880s, in England too. Middle and upper-class golfers increasingly saw St Andrews as a desirable place for a golfing holiday. Though some wives and daughters took up the game, golfers' families, and many non-golfers too, looked to the town's other attractions, particularly its facilities for sea bathing.

To meet increased demand, particularly in the holiday season, facilities for both golf and dooking were greatly extended. In the boom years of the late 19th and early 20th centuries, new golf courses were constructed – the New in 1895, the Jubilee originally for ladies and beginners two years later, and the Eden in 1914. Today there are seven courses. The seabathing enthusiasts also had their needs catered for, with St Andrews Town Council constructing tidal swimming ponds and changing facilities for males in 1902 and for women two years later. It took until 1929 before the Town Council conceded demands that mixed bathing be permitted at its Step Rock Pool. In its heyday from the 1930s until the 1950s, the 'Steppie' was a great popular attraction, when the weather allowed. For the bairns and their watchful parents, it was a safe playground; and for maturing teenagers and young adults, it was not just a bathing pond, but a social centre and a place where you were able to parade and pose before members of the opposite sex.

Inevitably conflicts arose, especially when attempts were made to widen the town's popular appeal by spending money on tourist-orientated projects. Some residents, not thirled to the tourist economy or with their own sectional interests, raised objections to noisy funfairs and troublesome pierrot shows. In the Edwardian period, for instance, sources of noise pollution, according to letter writers to the St Andrews Citizen, included Jacob Primmer (an ultra-Protestant preacher) 'bawling' on the Embankment, 'hot gospellers' from Oxford with a portable organ and services for children at night when they should have been in bed, and for two months 'the nasal droning of the Ethiopian Serenaders' (face-blackened pierrots). The ancient city, such critics claimed, was being transformed 'into a sort of 3rd-rate Portobello'. The better class of visitor, they feared, was being frightened away. Similar attitudes were expressed when fifty years later the Kinburn Caravan Park was expanded. In late June 1953 the Citizen drew attention to the slack holiday business 'during the past few weeks'. Some in the town, it reported, blamed it on the Kinburn camping site: in catering for the caravanners 'more harm than good is done to the community.' By August, all was seemingly well and the Links were back to a more healthy state of affairs. There was 'a noticeable change in the type of visitor now in the town'. As the Citizen observed, the July visitors were obviously not golfers and this had been the case for a few years past. That summer the number of Glasgow Fair visitors was estimated at around 3,000. The professional man, the Citizen declared in 1955, was being superseded, particularly in July, by the manual worker, and the fortnightly golfer to some extent by the short-term visitor. 'Lets of a month or longer for families,' it continued, 'are almost unheard of.' The number of day trippers arriving by bus at weekends was also on the rise. This for some was also a source of concern, especially if the excursionists were of the drunk and disorderly 'paper hat and streamer' brigade. But at least there was more for the visitors to do, especially once all Sabbatarian restrictions were lifted. The putting greens and tennis courts were now open for Sunday play and likewise Sunday golf had been accepted. For post-World War II St Andrews, there was, as we shall show, another cause of dissension – namely, the purchase by the University of hotels for conversion to student hostels. In the same period another contentious issue was the vexed question of what to do about the Step Rock Swimming Pool. It was not until 1988 that the by then derelict Steppie was replaced by the indoor pond at the East Sands Leisure Centre. Other recent holiday attractions opened in St Andrews also reflect the contemporary need for bad weather facilities. They include the St Andrews Aquarium constructed on the Step Rock Bathing Pool site, the British Golf Museum, and the rebuilt Abbey Theatre.

But it is St Andrews' atmospheric totality that is the greatest attraction of all – its historic heritage and traditions, its streets and closes, historic buildings, monuments and ruins. To quote the poet George Bruce:

Old tales, old customs and old men's dreams
Obscure this town. Memories abound.
In the mild misted air, and in the sharp air
Toga and gown walk the pier.
The past sleeps in the stones.

The author:

Eric Simpson, who is a former Head of History at Moray House Institute of Education, Edinburgh, is a part-time lecturer at St Andrews and Edinburgh Universities. He is a native of Buckie, Banffshire, and has lived in Dalgety Bay since 1966. His books include *Going on Holiday* in Scotland's Past in Action series (National Museums of Scotland), *Discovering Moray, Banff & Nairn* (John Donald), *The Auld Grey Toun – Dunfermline in the time of Andrew Carnegie 1835-1919* (Carnegie Dunfermline Trust), *Dalgety Bay – Heritage and Hidden History* (Dalgety Bay Community Council, and the script for the video *Auld Fife* (Forest Edge Films). He is the author, too, of the following European Library publications, namely: *Aberdour and Burntisland in old picture postcards, Buckie in old picture postcards* volumes 1 and 2, *Inverkeithing and Dalgety in old picture postcards* volume 1 (with George Hastie) and also the following with George Robertson *Dunfermline and Rosyth in old picture postcards* volumes 1 and 2, *Cowdenbeath in old picture postcards, Limekilns to Culross in old picture postcards,* and *Inverkeithing and Dalgety in old picture postcards* volume 2.

Acknowledgements

I am grateful to those people who loaned material and/or assisted in other ways. While it would be impossible to list every person who helped in one way or another, special thanks must go to the following individuals: Alan Brotchie, George Bruce, Gordon Christie, John R. Hume, Peter Gillespie, Cilla Jackson, Susan Keracher, Mr. and Mrs. W. Paul, Dr. Norman Reid, George Robertson, Owen Silver and Janet Inglis Sykes.

Thanks are due also to the staff of the following institutions for their invaluable assistance, and with reference to the four last named bodies, for their permission also to reproduce images: Fife Council Libraries at Cupar, Dunfermline and St Andrews; National Library of Scotland; Scottish Record Office; Royal Commission on the Ancient and Historical Monuments of Scotland; St Andrews Preservation Trust; the Department of Special Collections of the Library of the University of St Andrews; and the Hay Fleming Reference Library, St Andrews.

I am also greatly indebted to my wife Kathleen for proof reading and her encouragement and support.

If I have inadvertently omitted any names from this list, please accept my apologies.

The extract from the poem by George Bruce, which is quoted in my introduction, is entitled *St Andrews, June, 1946*. It is from *Today Tomorrow. The Collected Poems of George Bruce 1933-2000* (Ed. Lucinda Prestige), which is published by Polygon, Edinburgh University Press.

1 'Where will we spend our Holiday?' For artist D. Small and publisher Raphael Tuck, the message is quite clear, St Andrews was definitely a good place to spend a holiday. Black's *Guide to Scotland* (1907), too, considered that the town as a seaside place was admirable 'having retained a great deal of its primitive simplicity.'

North Street provides a picturesque scene with St Salvator's tower on the left and the cathedral ruins in the distance. Posting this card in Dundee in 1907, the sender was evidently confident that it would be delivered promptly, since he was writing to tell his girl friend in Perth that he would meet her next day. In the early 1900s post-cards were used to convey messages that nowadays would be delivered by phone or E-mail.

Where will we spend our Holiday?

D. Small

North Street, St. Andrews

2 Here we have a scene of circa 1900 date with a group of middle-class ladies and children at a section of the West Sands, which has obviously been set aside as a segregated bathing area. Unusually no one is looking at the photographer. The tents were for changing into bathing costumes. We must presume that these ladies did not want to be photographed in their bathing suits. Bathing areas were strictly regulated. In 1838, according to a contemporary plan, there were four bathing stations close to the town: at the Baths for ladies, the Step Rock for 'gentlemen', the shore by the Bow Butts for beginners, and what later became the Ladies Pond for boys. (*Photograph courtesy of St Andrews University Library.*)

3 Sometime after 1838 bathing machines were introduced to St Andrews and remained a feature of the West Sands scene for many years. Such machines, where seabathers could change, were an essential feature of the well-regulated resort. Normally a horse, perhaps the one on the left, was employed to draw the machines into the sea, thus giving bathers more privacy than would otherwise be possible. As with the town's other dooking facilities, the operation of the machines was supervised by the Bathing Committee of St Andrews Town Council. Latterly, the machines, or coaches as they were called in St Andrews, were no longer wheeled into the sea but used instead as stationary changing huts.

4 Donkeys and ponies on the beach were the bairns' delight, as we observe in this late 1940s Valentine postcard. This like other beach enterprises needed local government sanction. We find in the 1947 Town Council Minutes that H. Gray was licenced to put three ponies and two donkeys on to the West Sands. But he had to pay the Town Council £1 for the privilege and a further proviso ensured that the animals had to be inspected by a vet. Violet and Harry Gray who came from Kirkcaldy continued to serve the public, generally on the West Sands, for over forty years. Notice in the postcard the young assistants. These helpers were local boys and girls, who were rewarded with small sums of cash and free rides on the donkeys.

5 Evidently quite a few of the visitors to the West Sands, as we see in this 1935 view, had arrived by car or motor bike. Parking arrangements then were much more haphazard than would be tolerated today. The cost of parking, though, roused some ire, with frequent angry letters to the newspapers. Note the milk bar on the left, an early 20th century innovation. Many visitors are wearing long winter-style coats, no doubt a sensible precaution for such an exposed stretch of seafront. Hats or other headgear too were still de rigeur at least for the older generation.

THE SANDS, ST. ANDREWS.

ST. ANDREWS FROM THE WEST SANDS.

6 From 1909 till the 1950s motor bike races, including Scottish Speed Championships, were very popular events attracting at their peak over two thousand spectators. These events over a mile long course were held on the West Sands on Saturdays by permission of the Town Council. The list of bikes recall a long gone era when competitors rode mainly British-made models like Norton, BSA, Matchless, Triumph and Velocette.

7 As well as national organizations like the Scottish Auto-Cycle Union (programme illustrated here), local societies like the St Andrews and District Motor Club also organized events, with a number of local men, and on at least one occasion a lady too, racing on the sands. Usually a number of local riders participated in these events. Bike No. 1, illustrated here, was a composite machine assembled by a local rider. Motor car races were also held on the West Sands but, as a former competitor told me, the bikes were more popular as they provided more thrills and spills. But he could recall only one fatality when a spectator was killed during a Friday night practice run. For the Saturday events the racing area was roped off.

Scottish Motor Cycle Speed Championships

(Organised by and Under the Open Competition Rules of the Scottish Auto-Cycle Union).

On the WEST SANDS, ST. ANDREWS
SATURDAY, 14th JULY, 1928

At 3 p.m.   Machines to be presented at 2 p.m.

Official Programme - 3d.

HAY NISBET & CO. LTD., PRINTERS, GLASGOW.

8 The Citizen reported in July 1950 that for the annual motor car races organized by the Lothian Car Club several thousand spectators lined almost the full length of the West Sands. The 10-mile handicap race was won by a promising young Edinburgh driver, Ron Flockhart, in his MG car. This was one driver who did fulfill his early promise. One car, we are told, was recorded at speeds up to 115 miles per hour on the straights, the highest ever at St Andrews. The trophies were presented by a well-known film star of the day, Jean Kent. *Her Favourite Husband* and *The Browning Version* were the films she starred in that year. (Photograph: Cowie Collection courtesy of St Andrews University Library.)

9 The Victorians had encouraged swimming as one of the desirable manly sports and the Step Rock had long been a favoured spot for male bathers 'of all classes and ages.' In this very early image (July 1887), we see a very basic shelter — canvas sheeting on a metal framework. Circa 1870 the Step Rock was the location for the annual races, which were held in July while the schools were in session. To start the race, competitors dived off boats, having been rowed out seaward to the starting point. The announcer for the various events was the town bellman. There were no female participants. Although the races were organized by the so-called Humane Society, the day was always concluded with a duck hunt — with a real duck!

(Photograph: courtesy of the Hay Fleming Reference Library housed at St Andrews University Library.)

10 Since the Step Rock was an area reserved for male dookers, scanty slips were deemed appropriate wear. Women and young children, of course, had their own segregated spots. The Town Council, considering these facilities inadequate, sent a deputation in 1902 to Aberdeen and Peterhead to view the indoor and outdoor bathing facilities in these two towns. In the following year the Council borrowed £1,000 to pay for a new Step Rock pond. A bathing pool was built with enclosing walls supplementing existing barriers formed by two parallel rows of outcropping rock.

This partially artificial pond was flushed by tidal action. The Council considerately added a shower and douche bath but charged dookers an extra one old penny for the privilege.

11 To mark the official opening of the new pond in July 1903, a gala was held which attracted three to four thousand spectators. The Artillery Brass Band provided the music and the 'aquatic display', arranged by the Bathing Committee of the Town Council, included a water polo match and a demonstration rescue of a 'drowning man' by the fully-clothed 'rescue man.' The 'rescue man', a Mr. Malloch, was a Town Council appointee whose day, which was 12 to 14 hours long, commenced at 6 a.m.! They were hardy folk in those days!

12 This secluded ladies' bathing station was located west of the Castle, below the 'Public Baths', an indoor establishment, dating back to 1810, which provided hot and cold sea-water baths with water pumped straight from the sea. In 1895, according to the *Citizen*, a sea wall had been erected creating a large tidal swimming pond. Fifty people could also now be accommodated in the bathing boxes. Fifteen shillings was the price of a season's ticket, a substantial sum in those days, but for that the attendants also washed and dried and took charge of subscribers' costumes and towels. The re-equipped Baths was privately owned, but we find that by the early 1900s the Town Council had taken responsibility for running it. The whole concern was taken over by St. Leonard's School in 1920, and subsequently demolished. (*Photograph: courtesy of St Andrews Preservation Trust.*)

13 In December 1902 the Bathing Committee of the Town Council decided to investigate the feasibility of building a small low-water swimming pool at the Castle, a long-established ladies' dooking place. The success of the male bathing station at the Step Rock encouraged the Town Council to proceed, and in 1904 the Castle Pool was ready for use. A suggestion that mixed bathing be permitted at the new pond was vetoed, the more cautious councillors contending that 'they were not so far advanced as that in St Andrews.' The attendant was paid fifteen shillings a week, with the right to hire out towels and 'bathing dresses' as an additional perk. The pavilion, built into the lee of the cliffs, has long disappeared. With the introduction of mixed bathing at the Steppie, the Ladies' Pool became redundant. In 1950 plans to reopen it as a privately-run pool were rejected by the Town Council.

The Castle, St. Andrews.

14 In early June 1929 the Town Council, after some local pressure, rather gingerly decided to permit mixed bathing, but not till July and only at fixed hours. One consequence was the upgrading of the Step Rock pool and the construction of more commodious shelters and changing huts, also 'special sunbathing tiers.' This Valentine's postcard shows the kind of crowds that assembled at the Steppie on fine summer days. In the 1935 season approximately 45,000 bathers were recorded. Periodically plans to further improve the pond were brought before St Andrews Town Council. In 1955, for instance, the issue was debated in the local press. Complaints included: 'a relic of a bygone age'; 'exposed to the full fury of the elements ... and to the vagaries of the various sewers in the proximity.' Although the Steppie was closed in 1981, the indoor pond was not completed till 1988. The St Andrews Aquarium, opened in 1989, now occupies the site.

STEP ROCK BATHING POOL, ST. ANDREWS.   B.859.

15 From being a minority interest, golf had by the 1880s become a fashionable sport with the British upper-class with the middle-classes quickly following suit. By the late 19th century, as this illustration shows, the game was attracting sizeable crowds of spectators. Being recognized as the 'home of golf' gave St Andrews a considerable boost and the game's popularity meant that hoteliers and retailers had the advantage, compared with most other watering places, of a longer season. Others who benefited from the golf boom were club and ball makers and those who had enough skill to turn professional. The caddies of those days, many of them former fishermen, were, however, at the bottom of the financial and social scale.

16 As more golfers flocked to the town, so pressure grew to build more courses such as the New Course, which was opened in 1895, and here features on a James Patrick postcard (postmark date 1904). Notice the tent at what the postcard caption terms rather quaintly the 'first teeing ground.' The Royal and Ancient Club built a wooden shelter beside the first tee in 1907. For some years in the 1930s the New was considered more difficult than the Old. The Jubilee, opened two years later as a course for ladies and beginners, was called by the unkind a course for 'duffers.'

ST. ANDREWS LINKS, FIRST TEEING GROUND. NEW COURSE.

17 'The photo is that of 2 champion golfers which you will have heard of' wrote Jean on this J.B. White postcard, which was posted in July 1910 to William Thomson, a Leith saddler. While Bob Dow is a forgotten figure, Old Tom Morris (1821-1908) was four times Open Champion and is one of golf's legendary figures. For long greenkeeper to the Royal and Ancient, he was also an enterprising businessman. He capital-ized on his and his son's fame (Young Tom) by selling his own-make golf clubs and balls. Adverts in local guide-books reveal that his 'first-class work-men' not only produced his 'Morris Machine-Made Balls' but remade old balls.

MR. TOM MORRIS AND MR. BOB DOW.

18   This illustration 'A Dream of Other Days' comes from the North British Railway Official Guide (1914 edition) which rightly describes St Andrews as the golf metropolis. The Edinburgh city man at his desk sees in a reverie the Clubhouse of the Royal and Ancient. So off he hastens to Waverley Station and soon attains the fulfilment of his dream – teeing off at St Andrews. This is a good example of the way that railway companies plugged the attractions of the resorts on their routes. The other illustration, a humorous cartoon drawn by local artist Cynicus from nearby Tayport, depicts a golfer's nightmare. Notice the old style of tee. Before wooden or plastic tees were invented, golfers, when driving off, placed the ball on a small mound of sand. Accordingly, a small box full of sand was placed beside each tee.

19 In this Links view, we can see what well-dressed golfers wore in 1921. Long belted jackets for both sexes and plus fours for the men were very much in vogue. Golfers used fewer clubs which they carried in narrow open-at-the-top golf bags (see No. 15 also). Until the 1890s clubs were carried loose. Until a few years before, golf on the Old Course was free to all. Visitors were first charged in 1913, but ratepayers in the town itself paid no fees until 1945. Not everyone even in St Andrews took the game seriously. Some would have sympathized with J.R. Allan who took lightly 'a game that calls for so much seriousness in hitting a ball over waste ground.'

ST. ANDREWS FROM THE LINKS.

85336 JV

20 Nevertheless, both directly and also indirectly, as we see from this early 1920s advertisement, the golfing industry was a source of considerable profit to St Andrews. But there was no golf then on Sundays. In 1948, after a plebiscite, the Town Council sanctioned Sunday golf on the Eden course. Since permission was granted only for the peak holiday months of July, August and September, it is clear this was an attempt, a very limited one, to respond to the needs of visitors. Local hoteliers and boarding-house keepers pressed for an extension and two years later all-the-year-round play was permitted, but still for only the one course. The arguments against included the usual Sabbatarian ones and the fact that large numbers of the citizens perambulated on the Links each Sunday.

21 The Ladies' Golf Club was formed in 1867 and a miniature course for 'small golf' laid out on the Himalayas – a bumpy stretch of the links once used as a bleaching green. In time the main hazards were removed and the course became, in essence, a rather hilly putting green. A 1909 Official Guide relates: 'On week-day afternoons there is often a picturesque scene in front of the Ladies' Pavilion. Here the elite and culture of the neighbourhood gather. Retired military officers, University dons, and reputed Yankee millionaires come and play with the handsomely-gowned members, indulge in a little mild flirtation, at which they are adept, or drink tea on the verandah.' While they retain their own private club with regular competitions, the ladies of the renamed Ladies' Putting Club do open the course to the wider public.

LADIES' LINKS, ST ANDREWS

22 In time, women, from the middle and upper classes, sought to break into real golf despite many obstacles. Other clubs for ladies were founded, the St. Rule and St. Regulus. The Royal and Ancient was, and remains, a masculine bastion with currently 2,000 members — all male, of course. When the Scottish ladies could hold their own championship in 1903, that was clearly a sign of the times. Yet in 1913, when suffragettes were striking at male privilege by cutting up golf course greens, a St Andrews newspaper columnist could suggest, hopefully tongue in cheek, that any such local offenders be ducked in the Witch Lake or suffer six months solitary in the Bottle Dungeon.

23 When in 1913 proposals were made to lay out a putting green on the Bruce embankment, there was some opposition. A correspondent to the *Citizen* complained that this plan would mean that the pierrots would be displaced. The majority of the population, he asserted, were in favour of the 'merry pierrots' who were 'a decided boon to St Andrews.' But the Town Council went ahead and in the following year the course was ready for play. By 1925 there were three courses on the Bruce Embankment, one at Kinburn and that same year the East Bents green was ready for play. This sport has now declined in popularity and currently there is no putting on the Bruce Embankment, the ground having been used for other purposes at the time of the year 2000 Open Championship.

PUTTING GREEN & SANDS ST. ANDREWS.

24 When in 1852 a branch railway line was opened between Leuchars and St Andrews, the burgh became a popular destination for tourists of all classes. As we see from this notice for a 1853 rail excursion organized by the Total Abstinence Society of Kirkcaldy, tourists could visit free of charge a number of 'highly interesting' places in St Andrews. Apart from the obvious historic sites, the excursionists could be admitted to Madras College and 'the beautiful and interesting garden' of Provost Playfair. This latter was then one of the must-be-seen sights of the town. Not everyone, though, approved of the provost's creation. Lord Cockburn rather crabbily criticised 'the childish and elaborate gimcracks that deform the garden.'

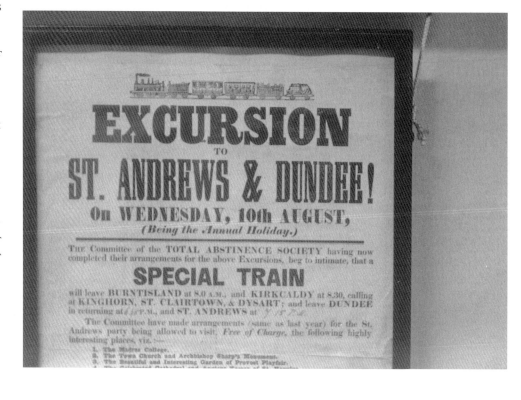

EXCURSION
TO
ST. ANDREWS & DUNDEE!
On WEDNESDAY, 10th AUGUST,
(Being the Annual Holiday.)

The Committee of the TOTAL ABSTINENCE SOCIETY having now completed their arrangements for the above Excursions, beg to intimate, that a

SPECIAL TRAIN

will leave BURNTISLAND at 8.0 A.M., and KIRKCALDY at 8.30, calling at KINGHORN, ST. CLAIRTOWN, & DYSART; and leave DUNDEE in returning at _____ P.M., and ST. ANDREWS at _____ P.M.

The Committee have made arrangements (same as last year) for the St. Andrews party being allowed to visit, *Free of Charge*, the following highly interesting places, viz :—

1. The Madras College.
2. The Town Church and Archbishop Sharp's Monument.
3. The Beautiful and Interesting Garden of Provost Playfair.

25   This and the succeeding photograph was taken in 1967 eighty years after St Andrews (New) Railway Station had been opened. That year, 1887, the town was connected to the East Neuk line which thus linked St Andrews to the east coast burghs and villages and more importantly greatly increased the flow of summer visitors from Edinburgh and, after the opening of the Forth Railway Bridge in 1890, from Glasgow and the west as well. The East Neuk line was closed in September 1965, which left only the short branch line to Leuchars. The town station, which had been well used until the Tay Road Bridge was completed in 1966, was reduced to unstaffed status in 1967 not long after this photograph was taken.

(Photograph: courtesy of John Hume.)

26 In 1967 the line was served, as we see here, by twin-unit diesel multiple trains (DMUS). To return to Leuchars the driver just had to change ends. In this photo we are looking north: note the bus station on the right. On the far side of the west embankment award-winning flower beds were once cultivated. Passenger train services from this station, which in its heyday boasted two bookstalls, were withdrawn on 6 January 1969. In July 1972 the Town Council decided that the station buildings be demolished and the site utilized as a car park. The track was filled in to platform level. Pillars in the west-side dyke mark the access point from the Kinburn direction.
(*Photograph: courtesy of John Hume.*)

27 Continental hotelier Johann Wilhelm Christof Rusack opened Rusacks Marine Hotel in 1887. This enterprising proprietor catered not just for summer visitors but also for winter guests by providing a reduced tariff and ensuring that the building was 'thoroughly warmed and kept at equal temperature.' The title of Marine Hotel was justified by offering hot and cold baths. As with similar establishments, the hotel's own horse-drawn bus attended all trains. Over the years it has played host to many notabilities including many world-famous golfers and indeed the hotel was recently remodelled 'to reflect the history of golf.'

RUSACKS HOTEL AND THE CUPAR ROAD, ST. ANDREWS   (23)

28 The Grand Hotel, opened in 1895, was in its heyday patronized by royalty and the upper echelons of society. Run down, after being requisitioned for military use during the Second World War, it was put on the market. The Roman Catholic Church wanted to buy it to use it as a Teachers' Training College. But this was the town where John Knox had preached the Reformation and a hostile petition containing 3,000 signatures was presented to the Town Council. The University stepped in with a proposal to buy the hotel to convert it into a students' hostel. Again there were objections, this time from the Hotelkeepers' and Boarding-House Keepers Association. This change of use, they feared, would be to the detriment of the burgh's development as a holiday centre. St Andrews University won the battle, and this once 'grand' establishment became a students' hall of residence, Hamilton Hall.

GRAND HOTEL, ST. ANDREWS.

Telephone No. 176.

ELECTRIC LIGHT.

Telephone No. 176.

ELECTRIC LIFT.

This Splendid Hotel, the most modern and best equipped, occupies the finest site in St. Andrews, adjoining the Royal and Ancient Golf Club House and overlooking the Links and Bay.

Apply: The Manager.

29   Visitors who couldn't afford hotels or other expensive accommodation sought rooms with or without attendance. It was, and still is, commonplace for tourists to send cards pinpointing their temporary abode. Jess, who had enjoyed herself 'A.1', wrote in August 1920: 'We are staying the fourth door down on the left-hand side of the picture.' She also informed her father that she would be back home in Stevenston in Ayrshire the following evening. This message was conveyed on a postcard that was date stamped 5.45 p.m.! Bridge Street, formerly Well Wynd, is one of St Andrews' many streets that suffered a name change, thanks to Provost Playfair's mania for 'modernizing and civilizing' the city that he dominated.

30 In the 1950s, as we see in this and in the following postcard, the Kinkell Braes camping and caravan park proved increasingly popular to many visitors, especially those with families, since a caravan provided holiday accommodation that was both free-and-easy and cheap. The Town Council had purchased the site in 1939 with water for cooking the only facility provided. Then, after the Second World War, starting with the construction of ablution benches and chemical closets, new facilities were added and the site developed to such a degree that it was regarded as an exemplar for other local authorities. A visiting journalist, writing in 1954, praised St Andrews' model caravan park where the vans were laid out in streets and the camp wardens, as well as collecting fees gave 'reminders on camp hygiene to those who may be needing a little guidance on such matters.'

EAST SANDS AND KINKELL BRAES, ST. ANDREWS.   D.485

31   The decision by the Town Council to develop the Kinkell Braes camp site 'to meet the growing demand for caravans' met with some bitter opposition. By attracting 'a new class of visitor' the Town Council, some critics argued, had changed the character of the town and had, therefore, rendered it less attractive to its traditional type of visitor. But others welcomed the new more plebeian holiday-makers. A correspondent, writing to the *Citizen* in 1955, approvingly noted how these July caravan dwellers and campers had banded themselves into a distinct community, organizing their own camp sports and weekly galas. Each week the camp residents raised 'substantial sums' for prizes. The caravan park is certainly conspicuous in this 1955 postcard, but at least St Andrews Town Council maintained a measure of 'tone' by keeping its beaches free of funfairs and obtrusive forms of popular entertainment.

CARAVAN SITE, PIER AND EAST SANDS, ST. ANDREWS.   S.1109

32/33 On 18 September 1903 great crowds arrived by rail to join the many locals who had gathered to see the warships of the Channel Fleet anchored off St Andrews. In this panoramic card we see the *Forth*, a Grangemouth-owned paddle-steamer, entering the harbour. The *Forth* was one of the many craft carrying trippers round the fleet. The writer (postmark date 14 October 1903) commented that the sea was very rough and added that 'all the people that went in the wee boats – well the fishes would get a nice feed that day, for every body was sick.' Several members of the Town Council, invited to Admiral Lord Charles Beresford 's flagship, suffered the same fate. Tragically en route to St Andrews, one of the warships had collided with an Aberdeen brig off St. Abbs. The loss of five lives and the necessity of a court of inquiry cast a damper over the fleet.

The Channel Fleet in St. Andrews Bay

Dear Peg, I hope you like this one,
weather the fine the Channel

Valentines Series

long ways in your album, It was awful misty
~~was~~ here and the sea was very rough, and ~~we~~

34 Steamboat excursions from the harbour were always a great attraction for visitors and locals alike. St Andrews too was a destination for excursionists from Dundee or elsewhere. In August 1897, for instance, we find the *Tantallon Castle* owned by the Galloway Saloon Steam Packet Company of Leith sailing from its home port at 9.30 a.m., then calling at Portobello and North Berwick before crossing the Firth of Forth and heading for St Andrews. Leaving St Andrews at 4 p.m., the steamer returned to Leith by the same route.

The *Renown*, a Dundee excursionist tug, was also a regular visitor around that time.

The Harbour, St Andrews

RELIABLE SERIES 804/8

35 Around 1910 naval-type uniforms were popular with the seaside entertainers, or pierrots, who performed, during the summer season, either on the sands or at the Bruce Embankment which would seem to be the correct site for this particular group, the Nauticals, and not as stated on the postcard caption. Rival promoters bid for the privilege of using the Council's stance. When the weather was bad, the troupes had to resort to the Town Hall, the Templar Hall or some other indoor location. Although summer visitors and many locals were delighted with this cheap and cheerful form of entertainments, nearby residents were less enthusiastic. Rowdy mobs returning from the evening performances, it was claimed, disturbed the folk who lived on the Scores. Their yells and shrieks disturbed and alarmed the 'residenters' who feared that St Andrews would be turned into another Blackpool or Portobello.

On the Sands, St. Andrews

36 Although pierrots were displaced from the Bruce Embankment (see No. 23), shows continued elsewhere. Here we see J.R. Tyrell's Nauticals, a company that had been playing at the Bruce Embankment since 1908. The card, sent to Alf Walters, a ventriloquist who was performing in Crieff, is dated 10 August 1914, just six days after the outbreak of the First World War. The sender jokes that he is writing since he has 'a few minutes to spare before the Germans capture us.' Adding that he thought that his party would be winding up earlier than usual because of the war, he wrote that, in that case, he could give his ventriloquist friend a 'turn' at his benefit concert. It is likely, though, that these young men would have been wearing real-life uniforms before the war finally ended in 1918.

J. R. Tyrrell's "Nauticals" St. Andrews 1914.

37 'Wee Willie' was one of the comedy stars of the circa 1910 shows and here we see his name (part only visible) adorning this West Sands booth, which had been erected by permission of the Council. A few years earlier the Council had tried to insist that lessees provide only 'high-class' entertainment in the form of instrumental and vocal music. But these performers had returned to the traditional pierrot style of performance and costume. Their dress, complete with pom-poms, ruff and cone-shaped hat, was derived from the Italian *commedia dell'arte* troupes. Those who had paid were seated inside the enclosure. Pierrots had to be skilled in the art of 'bottling' – i.e. extracting cash from the spectators, usually the great majority who had remained outside.

Once the performance was over the chairs were stacked inside the hut. The swing doors were then shut and padlocked.

61478   ST. ANDREWS FROM THE LINKS   VALENTINES SERIES

38 In this 1920s view we see an early Bow Butts pierrots' booth. After this simple hut was burned down, the Town Council rejected alternative proposals and decided in 1927, despite vociferous opposition from the Scores ratepayers, to invest in a new pavilion, complete with electric lighting and fenced enclosure. The lessees were to be charged £100 rent for the season – just over 1/5th of the estimated cost – and provide their own piano and moveable furniture. This building still stands, latterly serving as a tearoom/refreshment stall. Below the hut, a motorboat with trippers on board can be seen approaching the mobile jetty. But notice the gap between the jetty and dry land! Pleasure boats for hire, rowing boats mainly, had to be licenced by the Town Council. In 1928 James Cargill was the licensee at the Bruce Embankment.

39 When the Busy Bees opened their season at the new pavilion on 23 June 1928, they were welcomed, the *Citizen* tells us, by senior councillor, Dean of Guild W.T. Linskill. Everything connected with this talented company was new, this self-confessed pierrot buff enthused: new songs, new music, new dances and new dresses. We can see that these entertainers had discarded the traditional clown-style hats and had adopted the more fashionable close-fitting skull caps. Among the Busy Bees there were singers and dancers, a comedian and a comedienne who doubled as a male impersonator. There was also a Scottish character entertainer and a dancer who specialized in the nowadays strictly incorrect 'coon studies.' Since it was St Andrews, comedians would have toned down the more risky elements in their routine.

Mrs LEO BLISS'S BUSY BEES. St ANDREWS. 1928.

40   The latter-day pierrot pavilion with its stepped seating can be seen in this circa 1950 Valentine's aerial view. After World War II tastes had changed, however. The kind of entertainment provided by pierrot troupes no longer appealed. Alternative forms of entertainment such as ballroom dancing and radio contributed to their decline. In 1949 the Town Council rejected a proposal to demolish the Beach Pavilion and erect in its place a sun lounge. It survived with change of use to takeaway and tearoom. Variety shows held in the Town Hall provided a measure of continuity.

Visible on the left of the photograph is the New Picture House, which provided a more sophisticated form of entertainment and thus also helped to accelerate the demise of the al fresco performer.

ST. ANDREWS FROM THE AIR

B 6922

41   The City Brass Band (in later years it was Silver) had for many years entertained residents and visitors alike with their Saturday evening open-air concerts on the Links and in return received some financial assistance from the Town Council. Simultaneously, concerts and dramatic entertainments (these conducted by the irrepressible W.T. Linskill) were held to raise funds to pay for a roofed-over band kiosk. Eventually in 1904 the Town Council, after considerable argument as to the most suitable location, decided to erect a bandstand on the Bow Butts and this was duly achieved in the following year. The Sabbatarian majority on the Town Council at that time, however, insisted that there would be no Sunday concerts.

BOW BUTTS.   [J. Fairweather.

42 The Byre Theatre, founded in 1933 by a group of young men and women inspired by A.B. Paterson, provided dramatic performances that were often of a high standard. Despite its tiny stage and a mere 74-seater auditorium and inadequate facilities, amateur and, from 1940, professional actors and actresses put on a full programme of plays a year. With a season extending from April until the end of December, the Byre also catered for summer visitors. The company also put on summer repertory plays in the Town Hall. The Old Byre closed in 1969 and the buildings were demolished.

43   Last century cows were often seen, being led out of the former Abbey Street Dairy and then driven through the streets to reach nearby pastures. In this photograph the dairy farm origins of the Old Byre are clearly evident. The entrance was on the right. Access to the dressing rooms located in the pantile-roofed loft, left, was by an old ship's ladder, salvaged from a West Fife shipbreaking yard. The theatre sign acknowledges, in small print wording, the company's origins as the St Andrews Play Club. The building on the extreme right was the workshop area. The New Byre (1970) continued the traditions of the old, but that building too became outmoded and was closed in 1996. With its two auditoria, bars and restaurant, the latest theatre, which opened in June 2001, is a much more sophisticated edifice.

'BYRE THEATRE', ST. ANDREWS

44 Entertainment for summer visitors, organized by the St Andrews Publicity and Information Service, was also provided by the town's school children and youth organizations. This particular event in the Castle courtyard took place on 12 June 1954. According to the *Citizen*, an exceptionally large crowd enjoyed displays of drill and folk dancing, including the Highland Fling, by children from the Burgh School. Observe the maypole in the centre which had been used by the Primary III class for 'an interesting and intricate' maypole dance. The Boys' Brigade Pipe Band was another popular item on the programme. *(Photograph: Cowie Collection courtesy of St Andrews University Library.)*

45 At St Andrews Bowling Club visitors were heartily welcomed and matches were arranged for them, according to a 1930s Official Guide. The members of this private club, founded in 1887, were noted for their spirit of camaraderie. Today's pavilion is aesthetically less pleasing than the 1903 original, as illustrated in this postcard of circa 1910. Near here, twelve people were killed in August 1942 as the result of a German air raid. The Public Bowling Green in Kinburn Park was not laid out till 1949.

46 Any resort with pretensions had to offer tennis and St Andrews could offer this facility, both outdoors and indoors, since Victorian days. St Andrews Town Council, which had purchased Kinburn House and garden in 1920, extended the provision available by laying out courts there. The publicity-conscious Town Council also helped to bring the Scottish Hard Courts Championship to Kinburn, an event that attracted sizeable numbers of spectators. This tournament was held there every year, except for the war years, from 1923 until 1981. In this Dennis & Sons postcard, we see part of the bus station in the background. As the bus station was opened in 1954, this gives us an approximate date for the photograph.

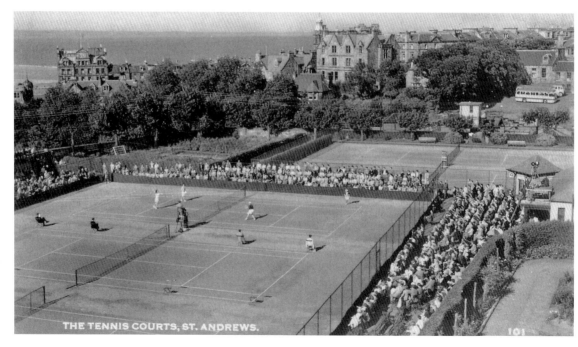

THE TENNIS COURTS, ST. ANDREWS.

47   The Lammas Market held in August is a longer-lived holiday attraction, and is one of Fife's three genuine historic street markets. (The others are the Lammas Fair at Inverkeithing and Kirkcaldy's Links Market.) This J. Patrick postcard gives us a flavour of an Edwardian fair day. At that time, and until the First World War, it was a significant event in the rural calendar, as the fair, as well as being as a carnival, served as a local feeing market where farmers hired their labourers. Notice the showmen's caravans parked behind the stalls. The showmen and stallholders bid for their favoured stances at a preliminary auction.

48 Another Edwardian postcard gives us a close-up of a typical decorated ice-cream barrow of the period with a carousel in the background. The bairns, standing nearby, would have had some Market pennies to spend. We glimpse on the Market Street-Church corner part of the window display of the Glasgow Drapery Warehouse. In the early 1900s, once the Market was over, the shows were flitted down to the Bruce Embankment. As usual, this brought a petition from the Scores residents for a ban on 'roundabouts and similar nuisances.' Generally, though, St Andrews folk had to make the best of their few days of brash and clamorous excitement, since the local elite made sure that there would be no mini-Golden Mile in their town.

49 This postcard conveys the essence of a true holiday occasion. Dancing in the Church Square was once part and parcel of this great annual saturnalia. Annie, who in August 1906 sent this card to a male friend in Leslie, wrote, uninhibited by her lack of punctuation: 'This is the band at the Market we had a grand day we were wishing you were here I had a few dances here but Auntie Jean would not go.' If she received a fairing (a Market gift) from a young man, Annie does not mention it. The Town Band precariously perched provided the music. But fashions changed and street dancing at the back o the kirk died out, although unsuccessful attempts were made in the 1930s to revive the tradition.

ST ANDREWS MARKET—Dancing in Church Square.

50   There were 145 fishermen living in St Andrews and 57 boats in 1881, which is the approximate date of this Valentine photograph. With all these Dundee-registered Fifie-pattern fishing boats it looks a busy enough port. The small cargo vessel tied up at the quay is the *Blue Billy*, home port Newcastle. Her cargo may have been coal or perhaps the cut timber or herring barrels stacked on the quay. The siting of the gas works (right) so close to the cathedral was a source of complaint until its closure in 1962. Part of the former Shore Mill (centre, next to the Mill Port) survives, renovated and conserved in the mid-1960s. The building in the corner of the cemetery, with a cross-shaped opening on the gable, is now a public toilet.

51 Now thirty years or so later we see part of the same harbour area from a slightly different angle. But the Gas Works lum is now visible plus, right, the tenements and storehouses of the Shorehead. The whitewashed buildings at each end were inns, the Auld Hoose being on the left. The sailing vessels shown here found it difficult to compete with the new larger steam-powered fishing boats and the harbour, 'a poor affair' inhibited development. The St Andrews fishermen gradually either moved to other ports or changed occupations. Quite a few became caddies or greenkeepers for the local golf courses. By 1929 there were only about thirty active fishermen left in the town.

52 The Shorehead and the area round the Lady-head at the east end of North Street comprised the traditional heart of the St Andrews fishing community. Near here once stood the Fish Cross, where the fishermen of former days had to expose their fish for sale before sending them out of town. In 1891, the date of the original photograph, this was still a close-knit and distinctive community with its own ways and customs. Often photographed, the fishing quarter and its inhabitants were on the tourist itinerary from Victorian days onward.

North Street, St. Andrews

53 As we see, the women-folk, in traditional garb, baited the lines. It was a messy task and best done out of doors. The litter and the smell meant that it was not too popular with the other townsfolk. The shell-fish used for bait was brought from the Mussels Scalps on the Eden. Belonging to the town and regulated by the Council, the Scalps were a signifi-cant asset. The lower-level houses on the north side of the street were demol-ished to make way for the Younger Hall. As, over the years new council houses were built, the surviving fisherfolk were dispersed and absorbed into the community at large. Notice the nearby gas lamppost.

NORTH ST ST ANDREWS.   J. PATRICK

54 This corner of the pier has always been a favourite spot for photographers. On the left we see part of the Royal George tenement with on the right the Bell Rock Tavern (now Bell Rock House). A horse-drawn lorry stands outside. There is a significant structure missing in this 1931 Valentine postcard. The postcard has been doctored, a not uncommon trick with this publisher. The Gas Works' chimney has been airbrushed out, presumably to present a more aesthetically-pleasing view. The Gas Works was not actually demolished till 1964. The Royal George buildings, long condemned, also disappeared around this time.

213645. J.V.   THE HARBOUR, ST. ANDREWS.

55 It is the same publisher and virtually the same view as in the previous postcard, but it is 23 years later and is a more genuine image. This time the big lum has been left in the picture. The lamp standard is still there but instead of a horse-drawn vehicle we have two recent-model cars, a Jowett Javelin on the left and an Austin A30 on the right. The bairns as always are mostly fishing or helping out on the boats. The wee laddie in the 'Oor Wullie'-style dungarees looks as if he has stepped out from the pages of the Sunday Post.

THE HARBOUR, ST. ANDREWS   B 9159

56 This 1948 Valentine postcard shows two of the rowing boats that were available for hire at that time. A few of the local fishermen had diversified into hiring out canoes and rowing boats and offering motor-boat trips round the bay. Board of Trade regulations ensured that applicants for boat stance concessions had to have their boats inspected as to their suitability. Since in 1948, according to Town Council minutes, only W. Chisolm's boats passed the initial examination, it is likely that the pair illustrated here were his property. For many years members of the Cargill family were also hiring out boats, not only at the harbour but also at the Bruce Embankment.

THE HARBOUR, ST. ANDREWS.

B.938.

57　Just as some fishermen adapted to the new tourist economy, so shopkeepers also recognized that they had to cater not just for their regular customers, but also for summer visitors who often had special needs and requirements. With no Tourist Information Office, shops, like McDougall's Grocery Warehouse, filled the gap by providing, as we see from this advertisement in a mid-1930s guidebook, lists of furnished houses, apartments etc. Such lists gave detailed information as to ownership, number of rooms, bathrooms (if any), and period of availability.

Clients from a distance were required to send for a list enclosing a stamped, addressed envelope.

McDOUGALL'S
104 MARKET STREET
ST. ANDREWS

All information FREE regarding
FURNISHED HOUSES   APARTMENTS
HOTELS   and   BOARDING HOUSES

Purveyors of High Class Groceries and
Provisions
Personal Attention.
Phone :
ST. ANDREWS 60———HOUSE PHONE 560.

Branch : 8 ST. MARY'S STREET
Phone No. 60 (Extension.)

Visitors Note.—Our St. Mary's Street branch is also a
Sub-Post Office, and convenient for houses in the
EAST BAY district of St. Andrews.

Page eight

58 As with other holiday resorts, restaurants and tearooms abounded. In 1926 the Victoria Café was one of several that could boast of a tea garden. In the opinion of the sender of this card, the Victoria was 'quite good and moderate.' Students too found it good value with soup and a snack costing a mere ten old pennies. One wonders what the clientele of the days when it was a restaurant serving luncheons and high teas would have thought of its contemporary makeover – still a café/restaurant but now possessed of a bar and beer garden and offering such treats as Karaoke Nights and Happy Hours.

CAFÉ GARDEN, ST. ANDREWS.

201951.J.V.

59   In the 1930s the Tudor Café in North Street could also boast of a tea garden, but it too has also changed its image and is now the Tudor Inn. Next door the Imperial Hotel has also changed and, imperialism as a concept being no longer fashionable, is now the Inn on North Street. It was, nevertheless, a go-ahead establishment, and once boasted phone number 2. By the 1930s it had come right up to date, having been fitted with sun lounge and cocktail bar, also running water in all bedrooms and interior spring mattresses on all beds. Nearby the new Picture House (1930) offered patrons 'perfect entertainment with perfect comfort.' The bus we see in this 1956 postcard was on a private hire.

60 St Andrews had some claim to being a health resort. In *Health Resorts of the British Isles* (1912), the town, 'dry and extremely bracing' (very windy in other words), was recommended as a suitable place for recuperation after debilitating illnesses for those coming from 'the relaxing, damp west coast.' If you suffered from a rheumatic or catarrhal ailment, on the other hand, you had to beware of the spring haars. Visiting valetudinarians, as well as locals, therefore, appreciated the kind of well-stocked pharmacy that Smith and Govan represented, as seen in this 1894 image. As well as being a high-class chemist's, this South Street shop could claim to command extensive favour amongst the best families 'as an emporium for ladies' toilet requisites.'

61 South Street was the first of St Andrews' thoroughfares to benefit or, according to viewpoint, suffer from improvements effected during Provost Playfair's time of office (1842-1861). Afterwards in circa 1880 the first lime trees were planted. In this 1903 postcard, we see too circa gas lamps, which ensured that St Andrews' streets were well illuminated. Note that, while the croon o the causie was macadamized, the fringes were still cobbled. It is quite a busy street scene, with several horse-drawn vehicles, a number of bicycles, and, always a common sight, some hurlies on view.

South Street, St. Andrews

Valentines Series   39239

62   There are no bikes to be seen in this Edwardian-period South Street close-up. But a sign reading CYCLE ENTRANCE above one of the entrances prob-ably points to a bicycle shop. This is the well-heeled side of St Andrews, a world away from the Ladyheid fishing quarter where folk spoke the guid Scots tongue and where the pavement was a place of work and not a fashion parade. Note the horse-drawn cab and the extra-large ornamental flower pot stand, one of a series. The lads on the left wear hard Eton collars and leather boots, the standard footwear for boys in those years.

SOUTH STREET, ST. ANDREWS

63 Between the two world wars buses took a lot of trade away from the railways. No bus stops then but the trees served as route markers. In this 1936 Valentine postcard, the leading coach FG9457, a Leyland Lion, is bound for Perth. Behind we have another of Alexander's buses, a 1935-model Leyland Tiger. This vehicle was converted to a double decker in 1943. The opening in 1954 of the bus station helped to alleviate some of the town's long-standing traffic problems, taking some at least of the buses away from South Street.

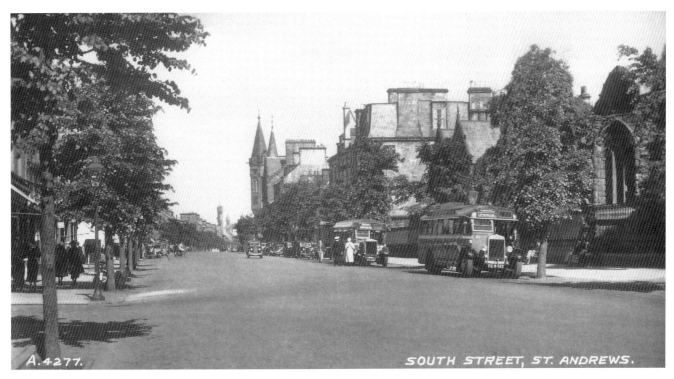

A.4277.

SOUTH STREET, ST. ANDREWS.

64 On the north side of South Street we see at No. 159 Coopers, part of a grocery chain. Margaret, evidently a student, sent this card to Pam in Bristol in May 1950 telling her to look at the Sphere and London Illustrated News, two upmarket illustrated magazines, 'if you wish to see some of our revellings in Rectorial week.' 'What a wonderful place this is,' Margaret concluded, 'and how lucky I am.' The Lord Rector elected by the students in that year was Lord Burghley, gold medallist in the 400 metre hurdles in the 1928 Olympic games. Ironically, in the film *Chariots of Fire* the character playing his lordship was filmed training on St Andrews West Sands for the 1924 Paris Olympics, but this like much else in the film is fiction.

65   Now we turn to South Street around the early 1950s. The building (left) with the words Christian Institute prominently displayed served as the Post Office from 1892 till 1907 and then, as the sign proclaims, was a centre for evangelical worship. Now secularized, it is incorporated into J. & G. Innes' next door. This last building was tarted up with Tudor features in 1927. Another nearby bookshop, Henderson's, informed visitors, in a circa 1948 guide-book, that: their Library provided 'just the right kind of holiday reading' with special terms for visitors; their Book Department was 'second to none North of the Forth'; and their Fancy Goods Department 'will solve your gift problem.'

South Street, St Andrews 28.

66 To the older generation Holy Trinity Kirk was known as the Auld Kirk. Going even further back Church Square was known, until the name was anglicized in Victorian days as 'The back o the Kirk.' The year is 1955 and the coach is a Bedford Duple owned by T.D. Niven of St Andrews. The number of charabanc or coach parties coming into the town on summer Sabbaths had greatly increased and this led to complaints in the press and heated discussions at Presbyteries and Town Council meetings. Drunkenness was the main problem with the situation aggravated with the law then insisting that on Sundays only *bona fide* travellers could have access to licenced premises.

THE PARISH CHURCH OF THE HOLY TRINITY ST. ANDREWS

67　Market Street with the Whyte-Melville Memorial Fountain (1878) in the foreground has always been a popular subject for photographers. Not much of a market here on this circa 1900 occasion – just a few pot plants and beyond that what looks to be a hotel bus. In 1910 the fountain was as dry as it is now. Speaking at the Town Council in April that year, Mr. W.T. Linskill argued in favour of repairing the broken pipes to allow the fountain to play again. The motion was lost, however, with Bailie Todd countering by saying that when the fountain was working, the water frightened the horses.

68 Now we have Market Street looking east this time. While, in this 1896 view, three of the lads by the fountain are barefoot, all wear caps and the one on the right is carrying a milk pail. The Temperance Hotel on the extreme left boarded 'parties' by the day, month or week at moderate charges and was, it claimed, convenient for sea bathing. On the right, the shops include the Fairfield Drapery Store, a Cupar-based firm. The Tourist Information Centre now occupies the site. This part of Market Street, as the name suggests, was the trading hub of the medieval burgh.

24250. Market Street, St. Andrews.

69 By 1956 the Whyte-Melville Fountain was housing flowers and the street is jammed with cars, quite a contrast with the previous images. Interestingly, all the cars and vans appear to be of British manufacture. In general, at that time few foreign-made vehicles were seen on British roads. On the right the Crosskeys Hotel, once frequented by commercial travellers, has been converted into housing accommodation, but the Keys public house retains part of the old name. The sender of the card, a holidaymaker, has marked with a cross her place of abode.

MARKET STREET, ST. ANDREWS

70 The message on this card reads: 'We are all sad at the death of our beloved king.' The late king was Edward I & VII and the postcard depicts the proclamation of George V on 10 May just four days after the death of his predecessor. The occasion was marked with great pageantry in St Andrews. The mile-long procession was watched by thousands of spectators. The platform party included Provost Wilson, the Magistrates and other members of the Town Council but, typical of the time, there don't seem to be any women on the platform. As for Edward, the sender would not have known that Queen Alexandra had sent for his mistress, Mrs. Keppel, so that she could see him before his death. Alice Keppel, incidentally, is the great-grandmother of Camilla Parker-Bowles.

Proclamation of King George V. St Andrews, May 10th 1910.

71   In this 1929 Valentine aerial postcard we see, at the foot, the roofs of the Shorehead tenements and also the incongruously-located Gas Works. Eight years later, Agnes Whitelaw chose a similar card to tell a friend in Paisley that they had had a fine bus run through and that they had procured rooms (at 163 Lamond Drive) within an hour of their arrival. Holidaymakers arriving by bus contributed to the eventual demise of the Leuchars to St Andrews branch line.

ST ANDREWS FROM SOUTH   207799

72　When in 1843 the monument to the Protestant martyrs of the Reformation was erected, St Andrews was still overwhelmingly Protestant. In 1836 it is recorded that in the entire town there was only one Roman Catholic family (one of Irish origin). Notice the old artillery piece by the Bow Butts and the early Step Rock changing hut and small boat nearby, presumably one of the rowing boats which were available for hire. In 1903, the approximate date of the card, a Dundee man, William Livie, held the concession, but he was instructed by the Town Council to cease Sunday hires because of Sabbatarian objections. This postcard was published like many cards of the time by a local bookseller, in this instance W.C. Henderson & Son.

Martyrs' Monument, St. Andrews.

73 This Photochrom (sic) postcard depicts the University students' post-kirk Sunday walk out to the end of the pier and back, an event that is in its own way a tourist attraction. The students' traditional red gowns certainly added colour to the town. For a number of years around this time, the late 1940s, the town versus gown clash was quite virulent. By purchasing a number of the local hotels for conversion into student halls of residence, the University authorities were accused of damaging the burgh's future prospects as a holiday resort. At the same time, though, the University by accommodating Summer Schools was also bringing visitors into the town.

74 As a winter health resort and, through the University, an established seat of learning, St Andrews was perceived as a suitable location for private schools. St Salvator's School on the Scores had been established in 1882 to educate 'the sons of gentlemen', preparing them for the Public Schools and for Naval Cadetships. A Royal Artillery Sergeant, as we see here, drilled the boys twice a week. In the days of Empire there was considerable demand for the type of education provided by St Salvator's School and similar establishments. A.G. Le Maitre, the proprietor from 1903 till its closure in 1931, took a prominent part in the protests against pierrot shows and other entertainments being held on the Bruce Embankment.

SQUAD AT GUN DRILL IN THE PLAYGROUND.

75 St Katharine's, the Junior School for St Leonard's, was established in 1894, seventeen years after the main school. The school with its gymnasium and emphasis on physical training was in advance of its time. When the girls were undergoing their 'drill', though, ties were retained and there was no unseemly display of flesh. It says something for the school ethos that a surprisingly large number of Scottish suffragettes had a St Leonard's connection. These included Louisa Lumsden, the school's first headmistress.

St. Katharine's ▓▓▓▓ St. Andrews, Fife   *The Gymnasium*

76 It is appropriate to end with a Cynicus card. The real last train for St Andrews left Leuchars on 6 January 1969 amid 'lively scenes', though not quite so lively as on this unconsciously prophetic cartoon version. As the communication cord was pulled five times on the five-mile journey, the train, though, took longer than usual. When the empty train finally left St Andrews to return to Leuchars, the passengers sang Auld Lang Syne and then gave three cheers for the town's own railway staff. Ironically, just six months earlier British Transport Hotels had opened a new hotel, the Old Course Hotel, on the site of the original St Andrews' Station and Goodsyard.